Machines at Work

Race Cars

by Allan Morey

Bullfrog Books

Ideas for Parents and Teachers

Bullfrog Books let children practice reading informational text at the earliest reading levels. Repetition, familiar words, and photo labels support early readers.

Before Reading

- Discuss the cover photo. What does it tell them?

- Look at the picture glossary together. Read and discuss the words.

Read the Book

- "Walk" through the book and look at the photos. Let the child ask questions. Point out the photo labels.

- Read the book to the child, or have him or her read independently.

After Reading

- Prompt the child to think more. Ask: Have you ever ridden in a race car? Do you think it would be fun or really scary?

Bullfrog Books are published by Jump!
5357 Penn Avenue South
Minneapolis, MN 55419
www.jumplibrary.com

Library of Congress Cataloging-in-Publication Data

Morey, Allan, author.
  Race cars / by Allan Morey.
     pages cm. — (Machines at work)
  Summary: "This photo-illustrated book for early readers describes the parts of race cars that help it go fast and win races" — Provided by publisher.
  Audience: Ages 5-8.
  Audience: K to grade 3.
  ISBN 978-1-62031-105-9 (hardcover) —
  ISBN 978-1-62496-173-1 (ebook)
  1. Automobiles, Racing — Juvenile literature.
  2. Automobile racing — Juvenile literature. I. Title.
  II. Series: Bullfrog books. Machines at work.
  TL236.M45 2015
  629.228—dc23
                                    2013044263

Series Editor: Wendy Dieker
Series Designer: Ellen Huber
Book Designer: Anna Peterson
Photo Researcher: Kurtis Kinneman

Photo Credits: Action Sports Photography/Shutterstock, cover, 4, 10–11, 12–13, 18; Beelde Photograph/Shutterstock, 24; Doug James/Shutterstock, 22; hxdbzxy/Shutterstock, 19, 23tl; Jon Feingersh/Getty Images, 21 (inset); Lawrence Weslowski Jr | Dreamstime.com, 1, 14–15, 23tr; Sideline | Dreamstime.com, 8; speed91/iStock, 7 (inset), 23bl; Steve Bower/Shutterstock, 9, 22bl; Steve Oehlenschlager/Alamy, 6–7; Steven Melanson | Dreamstime.com, 3; Transtock / SuperStock, 5, 20–21; Walter Arce | Dreamstime.com, 10 (inset), 16–17, 23br

Printed in the United States of America at Corporate Graphics, in North Mankato, Minnesota.
3-2014
10 9 8 7 6 5 4 3 2 1

Table of Contents

At the Track

Vroom! Vroom!

Race cars speed by.

People watch them race.

racetrack

The cars zip around
a racetrack.

One time around
is a lap.

lap

A race car is fast.

engine

It has a powerful engine.

A race car has smooth tires.

They grip the track.

smooth tires

A driver wears safety gear.

He has a helmet.

Buckle up!

A harness holds him
in the car.

helmet

harness

13

Oh no!

The car needs gas.

It's time for
a pit stop.

The pit crew runs out.
They fill up the gas tank.
They pump up the tires.
Then the car speeds away.

gas

MENARDS

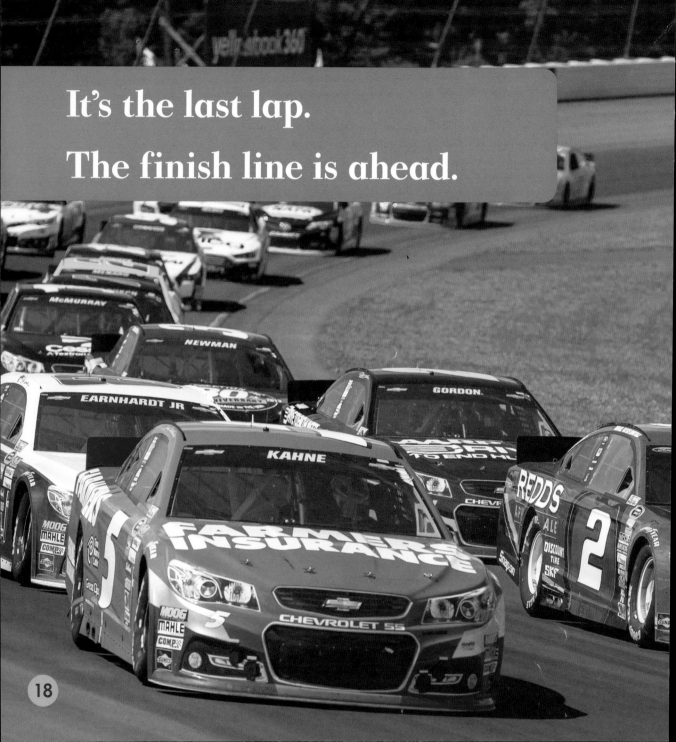

It's the last lap.

The finish line is ahead.

A checkered flag!

Number 66 speeds across.
She wins!

Parts of a Race Car

decals
Stickers on a car that show the companies that help pay for a race car.

window netting
The glass is taken out and cloth straps are put in the side windows to keep drivers safe in a crash.

engine
A race car has a more powerful engine than a normal car so that it can go fast.

tires
Smooth tires grip pavement on a race track.

Picture Glossary

checkered flag
The flag waved when the winning race car crosses the finish line.

pit
The place on the racetrack where a race car stops for gas during a race.

lap
One trip around a racetrack. A race is made up of many laps.

pit crew
The people who work on a race car during a race.

Index

To Learn More

Learning more is as easy as 1, 2, 3.

1) Go to www.factsurfer.com

2) Enter "race car" into the search box.

3) Click the "Surf" button to see a list of websites.

With factsurfer.com, finding more information is just a click away.

3126